# Ella in Africa

Mary O'Keeffe

**GILL EDUCATION**

**Ella** was sad.

Mam was sad.

Mam got up.

Mam got the box.

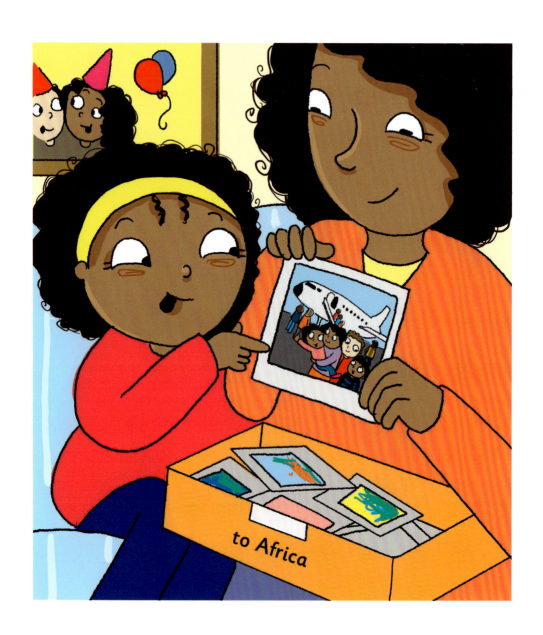

We got on a jet.

We got on a bus.

The bus was hot.

The sun was hot.

The bus said, "Hiss!"

Dad was mad.

Dad had a hat.
**Evan** had a hat.

I had the map.

We got to Nan's.

She fed us a lot.

Yum!

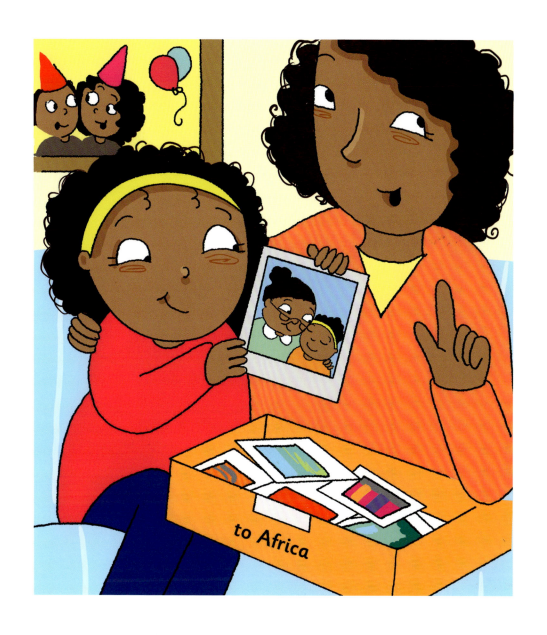

"I miss Nan," said **Ella**.

"Let's tell Nan!" said Mam.